BUILDING TOOTHPICK
BRIDGES

JEANNE POLLARD

DALE SEYMOUR PUBLICATIONS

Development editor: Robin Kelly
Cover designer: Rachel Gage
Artist: Carol Verbeeck

ISBN 0-86651-266-7
Printed in the United States of America
    20 21 22   07 06 05

1-800-321-3106
www.pearsonlearning.com

CONTENTS

Teacher's Information
Introduction   1
How the Project Works   2
Setting Up   2
Day 1: Introducing the Project   4
   History of Bridge Development   5
   Basic Bridge Types   8
Day 2: Forming Construction Companies   11
Day 3: Learning the Jobs   12
Day 4: First Building Day   13
Days 5 and 6: Major Construction   14
Days 7 through 9: Finishing Up   15
Day 9 or 10: Judging   16
Day 10: Awards and Bridge Breaking   17

Project Materials
Bridge Building Contest Rules   19
Bridge Building Code   20
Warehouse Price List and Order Form   23
Bank Checks   24
Balance Sheet   25
Boat and Truck   26
Planning Paper   27
Award Certificate   28

INTRODUCTION

Who says math has to be taught using paper, pencils, and books? Who says students can't have fun calculating fractions, figuring angles, and adding seven-digit dollar amounts? Most of all, who says youngsters can't be enterprising and cooperative at the same time? Not me!

Building toothpick bridges is a project with proven success. It is an inexpensive, ten-day project that makes math meaningful and real by allowing students to use arithmetic calculations and geometry to design, plan, and build scale model bridges. Working in groups of five, student contractors operate simulated architectural firms to create strong, economical bridges and account for construction costs. *Applying* math is key to the success of this project, which has been developed to apply and integrate some of the skills learned in math and science classes. It is appropriate for grades 5 through 8.

Traditionally, by the time children are eight or nine years old, the academic math and science curricula they encounter has abandoned the concrete elements of math to focus only on abstract concepts. For example, third-grade students may learn basic physics principles, such as how pulleys and levers work, without ever having a chance to *make* them work. And fractions—which are taught in about the fifth grade—are typically presented without manipulatives.

Most educators agree that involving the tactile sense enhances learning, especially if used to apply the abstract concepts learned.

Building toothpick bridges offers a "hands-on" approach for students to learn and apply abstract concepts, such as stress, fulcrums, the law of gravity, and the strength of different geometric shapes—even *without* presenting these concepts in their abstract form.

During this project, students will use the following math skills:

- Estimating spatial configurations.
- Estimating dollar amounts in the thousands.
- Adding and subtracting seven-digit numbers.
- Multiplying and dividing numbers of at least two digits.
- Measuring (using graph paper, ruler, and manipulatives).

The social skills enhanced by this project are equally important. Students will learn to write checks, balance accounts, maintain a task schedule, and work with others to accomplish a common goal. Working together on the bridge construction fosters a sense of camaraderie. In fact, I believe the classroom should offer more lessons in cooperation. I have found that this project gives such an opportunity; at the same time, it also generates the enthusiasm of a competitive game.

This project won't create future engineers or architects out of *all* your students. But it does help them see the world around them a little differently. One student said to me after the project's completion, "Bridges will never look the same!" In response, I say hurrah!

HOW THE PROJECT WORKS

This project is designed to take about ten days. In the course of about eight days, each team of five students will design and build a model bridge of wooden toothpicks, from specifications given in the contest rules and code. Each model bridge will be evaluated in a number of categories and judged according to criteria discussed later in this book. In addition, the teams must keep schedules, inventory records, and balance sheets of costs.

The first day will be devoted to providing some background information on building bridges. An introductory lesson is included under the Day 1 activity plan, but you should use your discretion to decide how much background information to present. Your students may be excited to learn a lot about bridges; on the other hand, they could be turned off to the project if you give them too much information.

On the second day, introduce the contest rules and code of the project and group the students into their five-member construction company teams. Each team consists of a project director, an architect, a carpenter, a transportation chief, and an accountant. The second and third days are planning days. On the fourth day, the warehouse opens to sell construction supplies and the teams begin building their bridges.

Building continues through the ninth day (although the project can be expanded if students need more than six days for the actual construction process). The company accountant must total their accounts and turn them in by the end of the ninth day.

Records of the accountant and the project director will be judged for correctness and thoroughness. Completed bridges will be judged for economy of design, neatness, and accuracy (that is, how well they match their plans) before they are judged for strength. You may wish to do this judging after class on the ninth day, with the help of other appointed judges (parents, colleagues, or the principal).

On the tenth day, the bridges are tested for strength—literally to breaking point—according to the guidelines on pp. 17–18. This is an exciting day for the students. I like to follow up the breaking activity with a class party to present the awards and celebrate the cooperation of all participants.

A word of advice: It works out well to begin the project on a Wednesday. This allows the architects to plan their bridge designs over the weekend. They will probably need the extra creative planning time.

THE TEACHER'S ROLE

At first, of course, the teacher acts as a general organizer. Throughout the project, the teacher is a cheerleader and, occasionally, an arbiter. On the fourth day of the project, the teacher becomes the warehouse manager. In addition, the teacher may be called upon to act as auditor. On the sixth day or so, the teacher becomes a building code inspector as well. Then on the ninth day, after construction has ended, the teacher assumes the role of judge. It's fun to wear a special hat to symbolize the particular role enacted. The humor generated can be quite welcome!

SETTING UP

Prior to beginning the project, give some thought to how your students should be grouped into their five-person construction companies (see suggestions under "Day 2: Forming Construction Companies"). Also think about how much introductory material you will want to present on Day 1. Gather the materials listed below for setting up the warehouse.

MATERIALS

- Flat toothpicks (about 125 per company).
- Cardboard (one piece, 15 cm × 35 cm, per company). This is for the base of the bridge. It should be uniform, without any bends. Thickness is not important, since ultimately it is the strength of the bridge, not the cardboard, that will be tested. If available, white cardboard is more attractive than brown.
- White glue
- Bottle caps, or other small disposable containers (at least one per company, plus some extras). These are containers in which the glue will be sold daily.
- Thread. This is for suspension cable, in case some students decide to build suspension bridges. Given the specifications in the contest rules and code, such bridges should *not* be possible. However, I encourage companies to negotiate with me for alterations to the specification, thus allowing them the challenge of suspension bridge designs. If you negotiate changes with any group, make sure your alterations don't hamper the fairness of the contest.
- Metric rulers.
- Wax paper (one sheet, about 30 cm × 40 cm, per company).
- Calculator (preferably two) for use during bridge breaking ceremony.
- Coffee can or small cardboard bucket.
- Metric weights (or objects that can be marked with specified weights; see discussion on page 17).
- Large manila envelopes (one per company).
- Warehouse Price List poster (based on the prices given on page 23).
- OPEN/CLOSED sign for warehouse.

The students can help you prepare some of these materials while you talk about the project informally with them. For example, they can help you bundle the toothpicks in groups of ten and bind them with masking tape for distribution ease. Enlist a couple of students to decorate a sign for the warehouse; the sign should read "OPEN" on one side and "CLOSED" on the reverse. Another student can prepare the large price list poster that you will need for display at the warehouse. For this purpose, provide poster board and the materials price list on page 23.

REPRODUCIBLE MATERIALS

You may find it most convenient to reproduce, before beginning the project, all the handouts and materials you will need in the course of the project. If so, you will want to prepare the following:

- Copies of the bridge pictures (pp. 6–7 and 9–10) as desired; one for each student or as transparencies for the overhead projector.
- One copy of the contest rules (p. 19) and the contest code (p. 20) for each student.
- One copy of the job duties and schedule (pp. 21–22) and the balance sheet (p. 25) for each construction company.
- Ten copies of the warehouse order form (p. 23) for each company.
- Two copies of the blank checks (p. 24) for each company. If possible, use real but obsolete blank checks (donated by the students' parents or school faculty members) instead of these duplicated checks. Just cut off or obliterate the numbers from the bottom of the real checks before issuing them; students appreciate the added reality.
- Four copies of 1-cm graph paper (p. 27) for each company, plus some extra.
- Two boats and two trucks (p. 26), copied onto tagboard for sturdiness.
- Copies of the award certificate (p. 28); the number needed will vary (see the discussion of judging, page 16, for guidance).

DAY 1: INTRODUCING THE PROJECT

Main Activity: Provide a general introduction to bridge building.

Preparation: Collect pictures and diagrams of different types of bridges; your class encyclopedia may be a good source. The pictures on the following pages can be used as handouts or prepared for use on the overhead projector. Familiarize yourself with the background material on bridges in the next six pages. Check to see what books about bridge building are available in your class library.

It's helpful to begin the project by covering some basics of bridge building. Providing an historical perspective may generate enthusiasm. The project may take on a great deal of meaning for students who imagine the results of their engineering task in the same vein as famous bridges in the world.

It is also important to point out the different bridge types and the reasons why an engineer chooses a particular design for a bridge. (This is really an interdisciplinary lesson in environmental studies, geography, history, physics, and mathematics!) Unlike real engineers, your students will not have to consider environmental or geographic conditions. In addition, all participants are given the same criteria (bridge length, minimum height, "foundation," and materials) for the task. Thus, their choice of bridge type will be largely a matter of creativity and economy; even so, knowing the basic types gives them an important frame of reference. It should become

clear, for example, that the suspension bridge is an unrealistic (though not impossible) choice, given the contest limitations. If your students learn these fundamentals of bridge building, they not only will better understand the contest limitations, but also will be able to classify familiar bridges and understand how they function.

It works well to accompany your explanation of bridge types with a simple discussion of the basic physics principles that create those bridge type differences. This discussion won't necessarily help the student bridge builders in their task, but it will help them see their finished projects in terms of real bridges. Learning these principles may also help them analyze why a toothpick bridge they are building won't work according to plans, or why a finished bridge fails to support much weight.

Day 1, then, is the time to present a history of bridge development, to analyze the different basic bridge types, and to explain how bridges work. The following pages can help. You might show the illustrations (using an overhead projector or handouts) while discussing the information about bridges—their history (p. 5) and basic types (p. 8). Some alternatives for introducing this project include:

- Arranging for a civil engineer to share her or his expertise on bridge building.
- Compiling and presenting a slide show of famous and/or familiar local bridges.
- Bringing several library picture books (aimed at young audiences) on the subject of bridges and bridge building.

HISTORY OF BRIDGE DEVELOPMENT

Basic bridge designs are developed from natural bridges—a tree trunk that has fallen across a stream, vines hanging over a river, or stones that make a stepping-stone path across a shallow stream. These natural bridges were probably built upon by ancient bridge builders. For example, someone may have built up the stepping stones, placed flat stone slabs or logs on top of them, and connected the stones to create a low bridge. This type of bridge is called a "clapper bridge." It is one of the earliest bridge constructions. Such simple bridges are probably still built today in many places. In general, though, bridge construction has changed greatly.

The ancient Romans refined bridge building with two important contributions. Nearly all of their bridges used the arch design—a structure that can support more weight than a flat surface can. Also, the Romans' discovery of natural cement allowed them to build strong, long-standing bridges. Many of these ancient Roman bridges are still standing today.

There were excellent bridge builders in Asia, too. Some early bridges in Asia used a cantilever design. This design enabled the builder to make simple, long-span bridges across fairly wide rivers. One famous bridge in China, built about 1300 years ago, is the Great Stone Bridge. Its graceful arch shape is not the same type of arch used by the Romans. Instead, this bridge is quite low, and the arch is very shallow.

The Renaissance brought new scientific ideas to bridge building. Leonardo da Vinci and Galileo developed theories about the strength of building materials. Their theories have helped architects understand how to make strong structures from lightweight materials. Bridge building became more exact as people began to use more mathematical theories about it. Another new development that changed bridge building was the development of metal.

About 200 years ago, the first cast-iron bridge was built. This was the Iron Bridge at Coalbrookdale in England. Before that time, bridges were made of stone, brick, clay, or timber. Eventually, wrought iron was used instead of cast iron. Much later, steel was used. Many new bridge designs were created and tested during this time. The Britannia Tubular Bridge, completed in 1850, showed one such new development. It was built from rectangular tubes of wrought iron. Similar tube sections are often used in bridges today.

Other important developments came with the truss bridge and the suspension bridge designs. The truss is an old design, but it was improved when engineers knew enough about science and mathematics to work out the mechanics of the design. Covered bridges were usually built on the truss design. Truss bridges were improved even more when metal was used. The suspension bridge was another basic design that was changed by the use of metal. The Brooklyn Bridge is one famous suspension bridge built during this time. It uses steel wires for the suspending cables.

About a hundred years ago, engineers began using concrete for bridges. A new method called "prestressing" helps prevent concrete from cracking after a structure is built. Today, most new bridges are made of prestressed concrete and steel.

Clapper bridge

Roman arch bridge

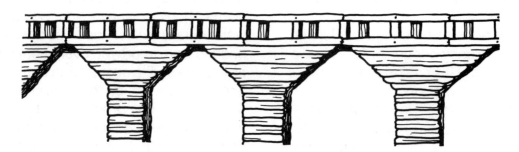

Timber cantilever bridge design

Great Stone Bridge in China

HISTORY OF BRIDGE DEVELOPMENT

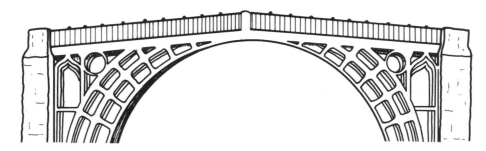

First Cast-Iron Bridge at Coalbrookdale

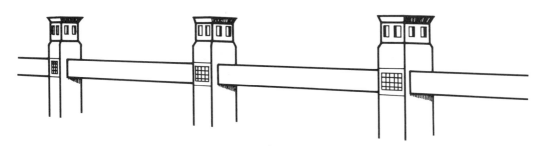

Britannia Tubular Bridge

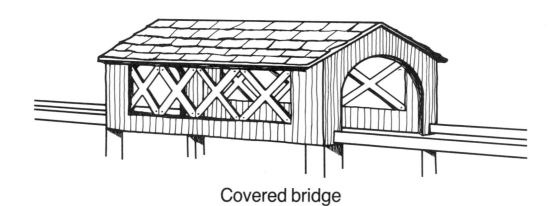

Covered bridge

Brooklyn Bridge

BASIC BRIDGE TYPES

There are three basic types of bridges—beam, arch, and suspension. Bridges made to be a combination of such types are called "composite" bridges. Each of the different types of structure holds weight in a different way. In other words, a beam bridge supports weight differently than a suspension or arch bridge does, and so on. It is the balance between the downward forces (weight and gravity) and the upward forces (the supports) that allows a bridge to stand and to carry weight.

BEAM BRIDGES

A simple beam bridge is flat across and supported at the two ends. A longer beam bridge may also be held up along its middle by piers that stand in the river. The weight of the bridge itself, plus any load it carries, plus gravity, are the downward forces acting on the beam bridge. These downward forces are spread evenly across the length of the bridge. The upward forces that hold the bridge up come from the piers.

ARCH BRIDGES

A simple arch bridge reaches across the river in an arching shape rather than straight across the river. Gravity, the weight of the bridge, and the weight of its load all create the downward force. But since the bridge is curved, this force becomes a downward, *outward* force. Rather than the force being spread evenly along the bridge surface, it is concentrated on the end supports. Some arch bridges have a series of arches under the surface. On other arch bridges, the arch actually reaches above the deck of the bridge.

SUSPENSION BRIDGES

A simple suspension bridge droops down between the two ends that hold it up. The droop causes the downward force to go *inward* as well. A modern suspension bridge has towers above the bridge's surface that carry cables to hold up the bridge.

DIFFERENT TYPES OF BEAM BRIDGES

There are several common variations of the beam bridge mentioned earlier. A clapper bridge is a simple, shallow kind of beam bridge that just connects "stepping stones" across the stream. A floating pontoon bridge is another kind of beam bridge, supported by the upward force of the water. Another type of beam bridge is the truss, which is lightweight but strong because of the open, diagonal (or triangular) beams along the sides. There are many different truss designs. Generally, the deck of a truss bridge goes straight across the river, without support at the middle.

The cantilever is a fourth kind of beam bridge. This kind of bridge is supported on two levers that are weighted by piers. The downward force at the center of the bridge is counteracted by the weights. This design allows engineers to build longer span beam-type bridges.

Engineers must consider many things before deciding which bridge design to use. They must consider how long the bridge must be, what it will be used for, how strong the riverbed earth is. The engineers also have to consider the effect of the river current (or ocean tide) on the bridge supports. Weather is another important factor. If the area is very windy or has sudden weather changes, the engineers may not want to design a suspension bridge, for example. The goal of a bridge engineer is to design the strongest, safest, most long-lasting, and economical bridge possible.

BASIC BRIDGE TYPES

Beam-type bridge

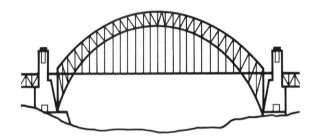

Arch bridge

Suspension-type bridge

Cantilever bridge

TRUSS BRIDGE DESIGNS

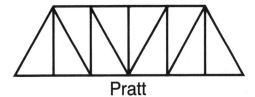

Pratt

Curved chord Pratt

Baltimore (Pratt)

Pennsylvania (Pratt)

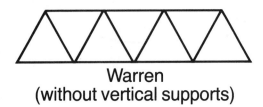

Warren
(without vertical supports)

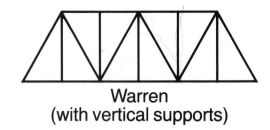

Warren
(with vertical supports)

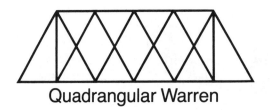

Quadrangular Warren

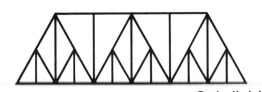

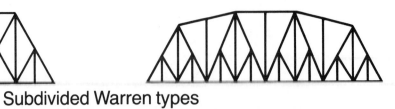

Subdivided Warren types

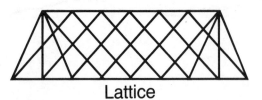

Lattice

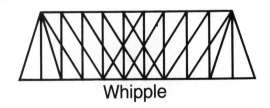

Whipple

DAY 2: FORMING CONSTRUCTION COMPANIES

Main Activity: Explain the project, discuss details, and establish the construction companies.

Preparation: Take one copy of each reproducible worksheet (pp. 19–25) for use with overhead projector (optional, for class discussion). Decide how to divide the class into teams (one suggestion is given below). Hand out copies of the contest rules and code (pp. 19–20) to the entire class.

Read the contest rules and code with the class and answer any questions the students may have. From one copy of the job duties and schedule worksheet (on the overhead projector, if possible), read and discuss the job descriptions of the construction company team members. By now, your students will probably be familiar with the warehouse price list (especially if they helped make the poster). You can explain the warehouse order form, price list, and balance sheet together at this time. An overhead projector will facilitate such an explanation, since individual handouts are not necessary. Try to take care of as many questions and details as possible before the project begins.

Now you will be ready to divide the class into construction company teams. By this time, students will be eager to form their companies. I think this is the hardest task of the project: I have found that allowing students to choose their own company members is not satisfactory; on the other hand, I don't like to choose for them completely. There is one equitable compromise, I believe, that allows the teacher some control but also lets chance play a part. The first step must be handled beforehand.

1. Classify the students evenly into five general achievement groups (the really bright students; the maybe less bright, but leader types; the students who need motivation; and so on).
2. Write the names of the students on individual slips of paper and put these in containers (by group).
3. Have the students line up in any order behind the five containers (one line of students to each container).
4. Have the first student in each line choose a name from his or her container and read the name aloud. Those five students called will form a construction company. Be sure to make a list to keep track of the teams formed.
5. This process continues until all the names have been drawn and all the companies are established. If your class doesn't divide evenly, keep the teams small and let some students assume double roles within their companies: groups of four tend to be more cooperative than groups of six.

When the companies are established, the company members should meet to determine who will perform which functions. Hand out the job duties and schedule worksheets and the manila envelopes. Give the companies about a half hour to decide on jobs, to talk about the project, and to take care of preliminaries. Each group should choose a company name and fill in names on the schedule worksheet. You will need to circulate among the groups providing encouragement during this time.

DAY 3: LEARNING THE JOBS

Main Activity: Meet with groups of students—by *job category*, not by company—to explain their roles.

Preparation: Be ready to hand out the order forms, the checks, and the balance sheets.

Meet the students in small groups (according to job category). Each meeting will last about 15 minutes. Besides reviewing their duties and procedures, there is another matter you will need to broach: it is usually difficult for some students to have limited involvement in the project. That is, some carpenters may resent not being able to design the bridges, and some architects may resent not being involved in the actual construction. Emphasize how important it is to cooperate and contribute the skills demanded by their tasks. If all company members do so, that company will succeed in its common goal.

ACCOUNTANTS MEETING

First, meet with the accountants. Distribute the balance sheets and the checks. Explain that each company begins with a balance of $1,550,000 in the account. Review their duties: writing checks, using the balance sheets to keep track of expenses, and so on.

ARCHITECTS MEETING

Next, meet with the architects. Review their duties, the bridge building code, and different bridge designs. Briefly explain how they will use graph paper (to draw side view, end view, road bed, and top view of the bridge—exact size). Suggest that architects use scratch paper (rather than the graph paper) for rough drafts of bridge designs. Discuss how they will have to estimate the number of toothpicks to order before the bridge is built. They will also

have to keep up-to-date inventories as construction progresses. Encourage creativity in their design task, but emphasize that the bridges should be economical and strong. On this day, architects will have to order building-plans paper from the warehouse, according to the procedure described below. Finally, remind the architects that their bridge plans should be ready on Day 4.

OTHER MEETINGS

Meet with the other groups and review job descriptions and duties. Tackle some of the logistics of each job without giving away too much information. For example, tell carpenters how to use wax paper (on top of graph paper) to keep the original plans clean. When you meet with the project directors, discuss leadership and cooperation. Emphasize that their hardest task will be keeping the company working together. Discuss how to maintain a journal, how to coordinate plans, and how to get team members to follow directions.

After these meetings, be ready to receive customers at the warehouse; you will have to fill orders for graph paper before the end of the day.

PROCEDURE FOR ORDERING SUPPLIES

The architect fills out the order form for construction supplies and gives it to the accountant. The accountant writes a check to accompany the order form when it is given to the warehouse. The accountant must have the check signed by the project director, then must give the check and order form to the transportation chief. Note that the transportation chief is the only company member who does business with the warehouse; he or she is the only one allowed mobility from the construction site.

DAY 4: FIRST BUILDING DAY

Main Activity: Conduct business at the warehouse and let groups proceed with bridge construction.

Preparation: For the warehouse's records, make one copy of the balance sheet (p. 25) for each company. Keep these copies at the warehouse.

This is the first building day. Have the companies meet individually at their "construction sites." Each architect will present the bridge design to the company and draw over the plans in permanent ink. Then, architects will begin ordering construction supplies. You may need to remind everyone about the procedure for ordering supplies from the warehouse. On this day, of course, the warehouse officially opens. Hang out the OPEN sign and the price list poster. Accept orders and fill them as soon as possible so the companies can begin construction.

Lumber (toothpicks), land (cardboard), cable (string), welding material (white glue), and paper are available for sale. A bottle cap is given with the first purchase of glue. Distribute the glue by the capful, but charge the company on a daily basis for it. (They need not complete order forms for glue refills during the day.) Rulers can be loaned out at no charge to the companies. The sale or loan of other warehoused materials will be explained later.

The warehouse should keep a confidential balance sheet for each construction company. These will be useful in case audits are needed, and also to check the accuracy of the accountants' records. When there are no customers at the warehouse, display the CLOSED sign and check out the construction sites. Wear your cheerleader hat if you have one. Try to find something positive at each site; praise the groups, keep the morale up, and try not to give any hints. The companies can usually solve any problems themselves if the general attitude is healthy.

Ten minutes before the end of the class period, announce the close of the warehouse. You may ring a bell as a signal, or just make the announcement verbally. During this time, the architects should try to figure out what materials their company will need on the next day. The architects' order forms should be processed as usual and turned in to the warehouse. Orders turned in toward the end of the class period will be filled by the warehouse early the next day.

The warehouse also acts as a bank. At the end of the class period, cancel all checks received during the day by making an X across the face of each. Then return the canceled checks to the accountants. At the end of the project, the accountants will turn in their canceled checks along with the balance sheets.

DAYS 5 AND 6: MAJOR CONSTRUCTION

Main Activity: Bridge construction continues.
Preparation: None needed.

The procedure for ordering supplies, constructing the bridges, and managing the company financial affairs continues as described on the previous pages. Eventually the carpenters will want to check the height and width of the bridges according to the contest code, using the tagboard truck and boat. These tagboard pieces are available at the warehouse and may be borrowed. (Filling out order forms should not be necessary for the loan of these pieces.)

If an accountant runs into trouble with the bookkeeping, he or she may come to the warehouse for an audit. If an audit is required, it must be ordered as if it were a warehouse supply; audit service charges are listed on the warehouse price poster. In order to discourage companies from using this service, audits are expensive. In addition, any company buying an audit will be disqualified from receiving accountant's awards.

When warehouse business has waned, close the warehouse and become the building code inspector. Take the tagboard boat and truck with you and check out the bridge at each construction site. Use the boat to test whether the bridge meets the height requirements; use the truck to test the width requirements.

During the course of the project, you may choose to fine companies for infractions or problems such as the following:

- Disturbing other companies.
- Leaving messy construction sites.
- Continually deviating from the supplies-ordering procedure.
- Building bridges that do not meet code.
- Handling bridges that are under construction by other companies.

Fines give the teacher a measure of control, but they should be used sparingly. Fines must be paid in the same way supplies are purchased. That is, the accountant must write a check, log the amount, and process the check as usual. You can, of course, set different fines for various infractions.

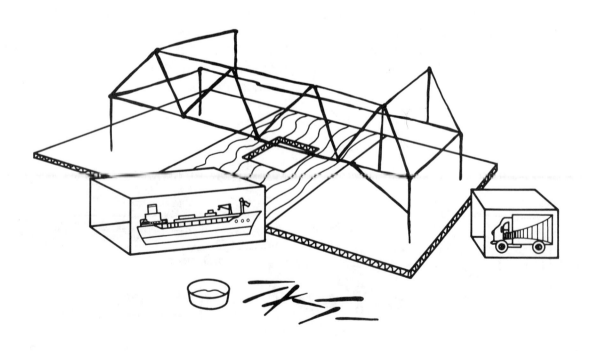

DAYS 7 THROUGH 9: FINISHING UP

Main Activity: Construction continues, while warehouse prices go up.

Preparation: None needed.

I. Saw Lumber Co.	Price List
Land	$500,000
Lumber	12,000 ~~10,000~~/piece
Cable	6,500 ~~500~~/cm
Welding material	1,000 ~~850~~/day's supply
Building plans paper	40,000
Extra paper	12,000 ~~10,000~~/sheet
Audit service	3,000 ~~2,000~~

Building continues on these days. Your task is simply more of the same: cheer them on, continue selling supplies from the warehouse, visit the sites as building code inspector, provide audit services as needed, return canceled checks at the end of the day, levy fines if you wish, and help keep the peace. Carpenters may get frustrated with their progress, accountants may grow confused with their own bookkeeping, architects may grow bored or annoyed as construction continues, and project directors may have an increasingly difficult time maintaining order. Try to keep the companies on schedule; the schedule may generate pressure, but knowing the limits will help reduce the company members' anxiety.

On Day 7 or 8, increase the cost of construction supplies and explain that it is due to inflation. The price of lumber, for example, might go from $10,000 to $12,000 per piece. Welding materials may increase from $850 to $1,000 per day. Cross out the old prices and write the new ones on the price list poster.

The actual effect of inflation will probably be minimal on a company's budget, unless a company has been especially slow in building. Even so, the inflation-related price changes make the project more realistic.

Day 9 is the last building day. Early in the class period, return any canceled checks you have received that day. Be sure everyone understands that by the end of the class period, carpenters will have finished their bridges; each accountant will have completed the balance sheet and compiled the canceled checks; and each project director will have gathered all written records—balance sheet, canceled checks, bridge plan, job duties and schedule, inventory, and journal—into the company's manila envelope and turned it in.

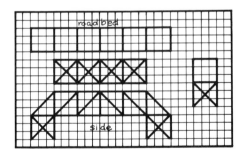

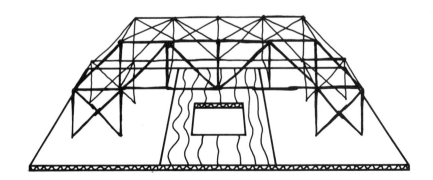

Main Activity: Preliminary judging in all categories except bridge strength. You will be doing this alone after class on Day 9 or before class on Day 10; students are not involved in this stage of the judging.

Preparation: Gather the blank certificate awards you copied from page 28. Select other adults to help you do the judging, if you wish.

THE AWARDS

The two major awards—for bridge plans and bridge strength—are presented to companies, not individuals. In addition, I give numerous special awards, some to companies and some to individuals. The number of certificates you give will depend on the results of the project. In fact, the award categories will vary depending on your class and their work. For example, if an architect is particularly creative in designing a bridge that is itself not successful, you might still give a special award to the individual architect. If a group works especially well together due to the project director's efforts, give a special award to that project director. Or, you might remember one transportation chief who was especially efficient. When you evaluate the company records and all the bridges, you will probably think of other criteria for making awards to different project participants.

THE JUDGING

Empty the contents of each company's manila envelope on a table and look at the company's records. Gather the balance sheets and canceled checks, or have one of the other judges do this. It may take about 15-30 minutes to check the accountants' figures.

Compare each balance sheet against the warehouse's records. I usually present a special award to each accountant whose records match those at the warehouse—*without* the help of an audit.

Next, look at the project directors' journals, schedules, and inventory sheets. In general, make sure all records are in order. Did any project director do an outstanding job keeping records? Are any of the journals noteworthy? This step in the judging will probably take a half hour or more. Again, share the task with other judges if you wish.

Finally, look at the architects' bridge plans and inspect the constructed bridges. There are three areas to judge for the Best Plans award: economy of design, neatness of the constructed bridge, and accuracy of the final constructed bridge compared to its plans. For the first area, simply consider the balance left from the company's budget. This takes into consideration how well the architect estimated inventory needs, too. Perhaps you will want to present a special award for a well-budgeted bridge. For neatness, look at how level or straight the bridge is. Does it sag? Was an excessive amount of glue required to construct it? Place the architect's graph-paper plans next to the bridge and compare the two. The Best Plans award should go to the company that built the neatest bridge according to an economical plan.

You may want to create posters honoring the winners of various awards and unveil them dramatically during an awards ceremony before the bridge breaking on Day 10; students always enjoy seeing their names in print.

DAY 10: AWARDS AND BRIDGE BREAKING

Main Activity: Hold the awards ceremony and the bridge breaking. This event will probably take an hour for six bridges. Plan to invite parents, the principal, and perhaps a reporter from the local newspaper—it's an exciting day!

Preparation:

1. Make a large chart—on poster board or the chalkboard—with the name of each construction company and a blank column to fill in with the greatest weight each company's bridge is able to support.

Company	Weight
1. _____	_____
2. _____	_____
3. _____	_____
4. _____	_____
5. _____	_____
6. _____	_____
7. _____	_____

2. Gather the following materials: weights, a lightweight bucket or coffee can with three or four pieces of heavy string attached (each about 18 inches long) and a short pencil or stick.

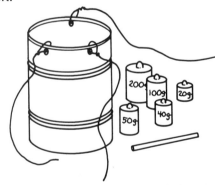

If metric weights are not available, collect various classroom and household objects (scissors, staplers, screwdrivers, and so on);

weigh them with a metric scale, and label them (using masking tape) with the correct amounts. Long, narrow objects tend to work best as weights. The various objects should have a combined total weight of at least 2500 grams; however, they should each represent small increments of that total.

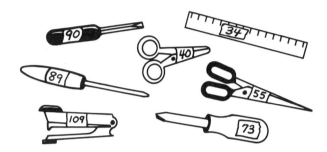

Also weigh the bucket itself, *with* the strings and pencil, and label it with the appropriate number of grams.

3. Have some masking or packing tape handy. Also, have one blank certificate ready for the winner of the strength test.

The awards ceremony may be conducted either at the beginning of the class period or at the close of the bridge-breaking ceremony. The advantage of doing the awards earlier is that the winning bridges will still be intact for people to admire. Present the certificates for the special categories and unveil any posters you have made honoring the recipients. You may want to make a special presentation to the company winning the overall Best Plans award. Other judges may help with the presentations, if you wish.

To begin the bridge-breaking ceremony, set up two tables or single desks about 25 cm apart and on top of a larger desk or table (see the picture on the contest rules). Place the weights on the large desk. If possible, assign an adult to work with each construction company. Each adult and each accountant should have a piece of scratch paper and a pencil. Now you are ready to test the strength of each bridge.

Tape the cardboard securely to the breaking tables. Tie together the strings attached to the bucket, making a small loop at the top with one of the strings. Feed the loop up through the square hole in the cardboard and through the base of the bridge. Place the short pencil or stick through the loop and across the bridge, where a deck might be.

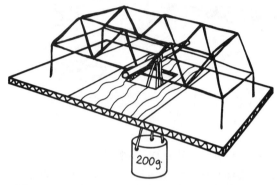

The company project director will hand you one weight at a time, calling out the amount. Place the weight in the bucket. The company accountant will use a calculator to tally the amounts of the weights placed in the bucket. The adult assigned to the company will also keep track of the amounts and will check the accountant's figures. If the bridge begins to sag or break, wait 30 seconds before adding another weight to the bucket.

When the bridge finally breaks, eliminate the last weight called. Have the accountant read the previous weight that the bridge held. Record the score on the chart. Each bridge builder will be contesting the highest amount recorded for a broken bridge. (Some bridges my students have made could hold more than 2000 grams!)

The bridge having the highest score, after all bridges have been broken, wins the bridge strength test. Write the company name and the winning weight on the certificate. Present this certificate to the company that built the strongest bridge. At this point, a party with refreshments is definitely in order.

EXTENDED ACTIVITIES

Bridge-breaking is never the end of toothpick construction for my students. Many want to try building suspension bridges. Some go on to build models of historic bridges, such as Old London Bridge. Others attempt designing ideal bridge plans for specific uses.

Students may also apply the skills they learned in this activity to the building of other model structures, such as treehouses, pole houses, or stilt houses for life over shallow water. House construction is more complicated, but it is lots of fun and, like bridge building, is a wonderful real-life project that reinforces many necessary math skills.

Student's ideas for construction are endless, and I encourage them all. In such places as these, dreamers and inventors are born.

BRIDGE BUILDING CONTEST RULES

I. The bridge must be built according to the bridge building code, using only materials supplied by the I. Saw Lumber Company.

II. The bridge will be judged for the quality of the building plans and the strength of the bridge.

    A. Judging of the building plans will consider neatness of the finished bridge, cost of the bridge, and how well the finished bridge matches its plans.

    B. The bridge will be tested for strength by placing a bar across the middle of the bridge and hanging weights from the bar.

        1. The teacher will suspend weights from the bridge according to the project director's wishes.

        2. The last weight that the bridge holds for 30 seconds without touching the cardboard in any spot (except at the bridge foundation) is the weight recorded for the strength of the bridge.

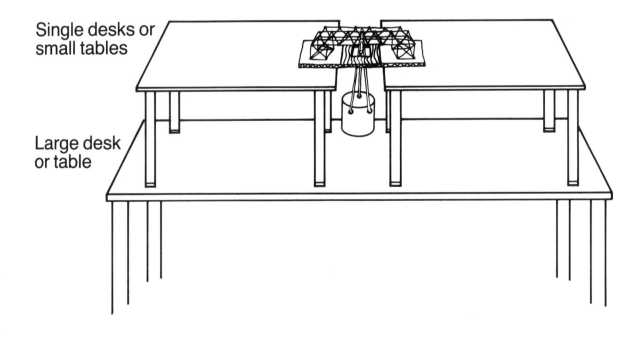

Single desks or small tables

Large desk or table

BRIDGE BUILDING CODE

1. Build the bridge on a piece of cardboard 15 cm by 35 cm (figure 1).
2. Draw a river, 15 cm wide, in the middle of the cardboard (figure 1).
3. Draw one 5-cm square at each end of the cardboard, 2.5 cm from the river and 2.5 cm from the edge (figure 2).
4. Draw and cut a 4-cm square exactly in the center of the cardboard, in the river (figure 2).

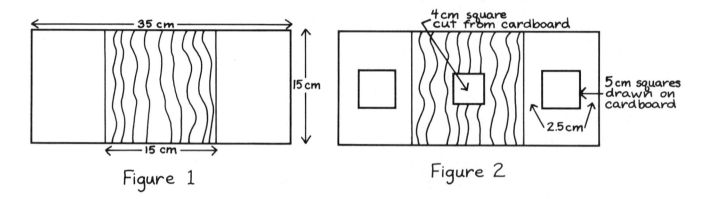

Figure 1

Figure 2

5. Draw plans of the bridge to show four views: the view from one end, the side view, the road bed, and the top view. The plans must be readable, clear, and may **not** be changed once construction has begun.
6. When building the bridge, apply glue sparingly **only** to join the toothpicks.
7. The bridge must at all times touch only the cardboard inside the drawn squares. Toothpicks may be glued into holes punched in the cardboard inside the squares.
8. The bridge must be more than 5 cm high. This distance is measured from the cardboard to where the deck of the bridge would be. The tagboard boat, 5 cm tall, must be able to travel the length of the river.
9. The bridge must be at least 4 cm wide. The tagboard truck, 3.5 cm wide, must be able to travel the length of the road, if the bridge had a deck.

JOB DUTIES AND SCHEDULE

Company Name _____ NOTE: Each company member may perform **only** the duties listed for that job.	PUT CHECK IN BOX DAILY IF JOB IS BEING DONE						
	DAY 3	DAY 4	DAY 5	DAY 6	DAY 7	DAY 8	DAY 9
Project Director Name _____							
Keeps this schedule; makes sure all company members do their jobs.							
Keeps daily journal of company's progress, recording any problems and their solutions.							
Signs and approves building plans, checks, order forms.							
Makes sure construction sight is neat and organized.							
Cleans up site and stores bridge each day.							
Cleans out and keeps container of glue each day.							
Keeps manila envelope with all company records.							
Does NOT build, draw plans, do accounting, or perform any duties listed for other company members.							
Architect Name _____							
Designs bridge and draws plans.							
Shows others how to construct bridge according to the plans.							
Keeps inventory of building materials on hand at the site.							
Makes sure actual bridge being built follows and looks like the plans.							
Orders supplies, filling out order form as needed.							
Does NOT build or perform any duties listed for other company members.							

	DAY 3	DAY 4	DAY 5	DAY 6	DAY 7	DAY 8	DAY 9
Carpenter Name _____							
Builds bridge according to architect's plans.							
Consults with architect as building proceeds.							
Supervises the company members who help with construction (transportation chief and accountant).							
Does NOT go to warehouse or perform any duties listed for other company members.							
Transportation Chief Name _____							
Helps carpenter build the bridge.							
Delivers checks, picks up supplies from the warehouse (the only one who does business with the warehouse).							
Does not write checks or perform any duties listed for other company members.							
Accountant Name _____							
Writes checks to go with order forms.							
Keeps balance sheet current each day.							
Makes sure that company account balances.							
Meets with auditor if necessary.							
Helps carpenter build the bridge.							
Does not go to warehouse or perform any duties listed for other company members.							

I. SAW LUMBER COMPANY WAREHOUSE
PRICE LIST

Land (cardboard)	$500,000
Lumber (toothpicks)	10,000 per piece
Cable (string)	500 per cm
Welding material (glue)	850 per day's supply
Building-plans paper (4 sheets graph paper; wax paper)	40,000
Extra sheets of either paper	10,000 per sheet
Audit Service	2,000

I. SAW LUMBER COMPANY WAREHOUSE
ORDER FORM

Order number _____ Date _____

Company name _____

Check number _____ Accountant's signature _____

Project director's signature _____

Item ordered	How many	Cost each	Total cost
		TOTAL	

CHECK NO. _____

_____ 19 ___

PAY TO THE
ORDER OF _____

_____ DOLLARS

_____ COMPANY

CHECK NO. _____

_____ 19 ___

PAY TO THE
ORDER OF _____

_____ DOLLARS

_____ COMPANY

CHECK NO. _____

_____ 19 ___

PAY TO THE
ORDER OF _____

_____ DOLLARS

_____ COMPANY

CHECK NO. _____

_____ 19 ___

PAY TO THE
ORDER OF _____

_____ DOLLARS

_____ COMPANY

CHECK NO. _____

_____ 19 ___

PAY TO THE
ORDER OF _____

_____ DOLLARS

_____ COMPANY

CHECK NO. _____

_____ 19 ___

PAY TO THE
ORDER OF _____

_____ DOLLARS

_____ COMPANY

BALANCE SHEET

Company Name _____

Beginning balance: $1,550,000.00

Check number	Date	To whom check is written	Check amount and balance	
			amount	
			balance	
			amount	
			balance	
			amount	
			balance	
			amount	
			balance	
			amount	
			balance	
			amount	
			balance	
			amount	
			balance	
			amount	
			balance	
			amount	
			balance	

BOAT AND TRUCK

Duplicate on tagboard or card stock (or duplicate on paper and glue onto tagboard). Cut pieces along solid lines. Fold along broken lines and tape each rectangular shape closed.

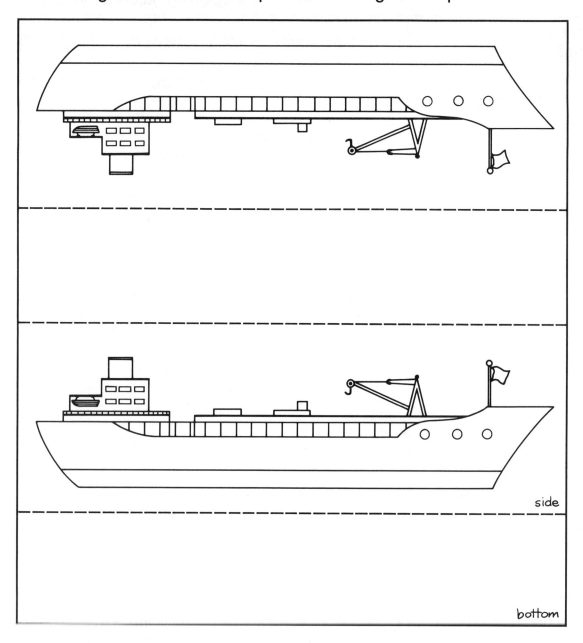

side

bottom

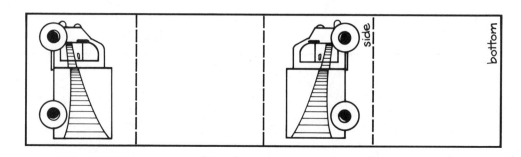

PLANNING PAPER

Certificate
of
Appreciation

Awarded to:

_____

_____

For: _____

_____

_____

_____

Signed: _____

_____

this _____ **day of** _____ **19** ____